WOLVES

A PORTRAIT OF THE ANIMAL WORLD

Leonard Lee Rue III

TODTRI

This book was designed and produced by
Todtri Productions Limited
P.O. Box 572
New York, NY 10016-0572
Fax: (212) 279-1241

Printed and bound in Singapore

ISBN 1-880908-33-6

Author: Leonard Lee Rue III

Publisher: Robert M. Tod
Book Designer: Mark Weinberg
Editor: Mary Forsell
Photo Editor: Natasha Milne
Design Associate: Jackie Skroczky
Typesetting: Command-O, NYC

INTRODUCTION

Even though their white coats would reflect the sun's rays and warmth, these two wolves seek the shade to escape the heat of a warm summer's day.

For centuries, the wolf has been one of the most maligned of all wild creatures. At various times in history, it has been venerated, as was the Roman wolf that reportedly gave suckle to the twins Romulus and Remus. More often, it has been hated and feared, as was the Beast of Gevaudan. This one wolf in the south of France was reported to have killed 123 people. Its depredations against people and livestock became so severe that in the mid–1700s, King Louis XV called out an entire army to hunt it down. It took 43,000 men and 2,800 dogs two months to finally kill this wolf.

European history abounds with records of the devastation of wolves on livestock and attacks on human beings. It is the general consensus today that most of the attacks on humans were done by rabid wolves. Single attacks could be blamed on rabies, but repeated attacks cannot because rabid animals usually die of the virus in a very short time. There are records of the Asian wolf carrying off, and eating, children in India. I found no mention of attacks on human adults.

There has not been an authenticated attack by a healthy wolf on a human in North America. The several recorded attacks were made by rabid wolves, which were killed and the disease thereby documented. It may be that because the Eurasian subspecies of wolf was exposed to man long before the advent of firearms, it had less to fear from man.

Wolves originated in the New World in the middle Pliocene epoch, about five million years ago, and had developed and diversified by the middle of the Pleistocene epoch, about one and a half million years ago. One type, the Dire wolf, was the largest wolf known to exist. A small type of wolf crossed into Siberia from Alaska, where it eventually developed into the larger, present–day grey wolf, Canis lupus. The grey wolf then migrated back to North America, where it populated all of what is now Canada and the United States, except for the southeastern section of the latter country. That area was populated by the smaller red wolf, C. rufus, which developed there. The United States government is trying to repopulate the Southeast with the red wolf today. The grey wolf was well established in North America by the time the first Indians and Eskimos came across Beringia, about eighteen thousand years ago.

Every wild creature was designed and adapted to fill a special niche in the web of life. We may not like what any creature does, but then no one ever asked us to. To paraphrase Gertrude Stein, 'A wolf is a wolf is a wolf'. Let us look at the wolves and then join them on their travels throughout the year.

Unless they are sheltering their young in a den, wolves sleep in the open throughout the year.

THE WOLF OBSERVED

The wolf is a large member of the canine family. It is not known for sure just when the divergence occurred that split the ancestors of our domestic dog, *C. familiaris*, from the grey wolf, *C. lupus*, but it is thought to have occurred about four million years ago. Early man was probably followed by a wolflike creature that scavenged on the remains of his kills. In time, the creature sacrificed his freedom in exchange for those remnants. The dog, for so the creature turned out to be, was not the only one to gain from the exchange. In time, the dog learned how to help the man in his hunting, guarded the herds of other animals that the man domesticated, was sometimes used as a beast of burden and, at times, even protected the man from other animals.

Wolves spend most of their time hunting, eating, or sleeping. After travelling many miles to make a kill, wolves usually sleep immediately after eating. This wolf, awakening from a deep slumber, is yawning and stretching.

The wolf and the dog are very closely related, as can be seen in the frequency with which the two species interbreed and produce fertile offspring.

Size

Most of the adult grey wolves weigh in the vicinity of 75 to 125 pounds (34 to 56 kilograms). Males are usually larger than females by as much as twenty–five percent. There are authenticated records of male wolves weighing as much as 175 pounds (79 kilograms). As large as wolves are, they usually appear to be much larger because of their long hair. In their winter coat, the hair on their back and sides averages 2 to 2.5 inches (5 to 6.3 centimetres) in length. Starting at the base of the neck, the wolf has a teardrop–shaped mane of hair that elongates into just a crest down the spine toward the tail. Over the shoulder, the

The maned wolf of South America is inappropriately named because it is not even distantly related to the grey wolf. In reality, this animal looks more foxlike than wolflike.

mane is about 6 inches (15.2 centimetres) wide. The hairs in the mane are 4 to 5 inches (10 to 12.7 centimetres) long and are attached to erectorpili muscles, which allow the hairs to stand on end, making the wolf appear even larger.

Extensive studies of the North American wolf species show that they measure between 50 to 70 inches (1.3 to 1.8 metres) in total nose–tip–to–tail–tip length. Of that length, one quarter is the tail length. In 1969, in Aniak, Alaska, I personally saw a wolf skin that measured 90 inches (2.27 metres) in nose–to–tail length. The fur trader told me it was the largest wolf skin he had ever seen in all his years of buying fur.

Much of a wolf's power to communicate relies on facial expressions. This snarling wolf is showing aggression, as can be seen by its exposed fangs, curled lips, and erect ears.

Wolves stand between 27 to 31 inches (68 to 78 centimetres) high at the shoulder. Compared to dogs of the same size, wolves' chests are much narrower. Their legs are also longer in proportion to their body weight than are most dogs. Because of its narrower chest, the wolf's left and right foot tracks are closer together than those of dogs.

Foot Structure and Speed

Humans are plantigrade, walking upon our entire flat foot, sole and heel. All members of the canine family, and the feline family too, are digitigrade, walking upon just their toe tips. Unless a wolf is lying down, the heel of each foot does not come in contact with the ground. The front feet of a wolf are exceptionally large. This is of great advantage to the wolf when it runs upon snow, as it allows greater weight distribution and more support to prevent the animal from sinking in as deeply when the snow is soft.

The wolf has five toes on each forefoot, but only four are actually needed. The fifth toe, corresponding to our thumb, has

regressed. It is now found up on the middle of the foot and is known as a dewclaw. There are just four toes on each of the hind feet. Each toe pad is surrounded by stiff, bristly hair, which acts as insulation and also provides a better grip on slippery ice surfaces. The claws are strong and blunt because the tips are worn off by constant contact with the ground. These are used for digging and in gripping the earth while running, not for seizing prey.

Wolves walk, trot, lope, or gallop. Their legs are long, and they walk at about 4 miles (6.4 kilometres) per hour. Their usual mode of travel is to trot, which they do at various speeds, generally between 8 to 10 miles (12.8 to 16 kilometres) per hour.

Wolves do not run at full speed until they get as close to their prey as possible. At that point, they make a high–speed chase to test the animal.

The wolf has five toes on its front foot, but only four toes show in the track. This is because the fifth toe, the dewclaw, has regressed. It has only four toes on its hind foot. The larger track at the bottom of the photo was made by the wolf's right front foot.

Wolves can keep up this pace for hours on end and have been known to cover 60 miles (96 kilometres) in a single night. They have been clocked at speeds of over 40 miles (64 kilometres) per hour for a distance of several miles.

General Appearance

Once a year, a wolf sheds its coat. The long winter hair sloughs off in patches in the late spring. The new hair that forms the short summer coat continues to grow just enough to gradually form the long winter coat. Although most of the wolves have basically grey coats, hence the common name, the coats usually have a lot of base yellow interspersed between the salt–and–pepper grey and black hairs. Wolves anywhere can have coats that grade from almost pure white to jet black,

This wolf has on its magnificent winter coat. Wolves shed their winter coats in late spring, and their new coats continue to grow and lengthen throughout the summer and autumn.

This wolf pup is between three and four months of age. Not until it is two and a half years old will it will leave the pack to find a mate.

This wolf splashes into the water without a moment's hesitation. Alaskan wolves often follow gravel bars and riverbeds in search of prey and constantly wade back and forth in the water on these journeys.

A trotting wolf is a tireless traveller. Wolves have been known to cover as much as 60 miles (96 kilometres) in a twenty–four–hour period.

A wolf that is bested in either a fight or in play will roll on its back and expose its throat as a sign of complete surrender.

although all of the arctic wolves are usually all white.

Wolves are very intelligent creatures whose upright ears, sharp, pointed muzzle, inquiring eyes, and other facial features instantly convey this quality. Their heads closely resemble that of a German shepherd dog, although the skull is broader and more massive. Wolves also have ruffs of long hair framing the sides of their faces like sideburns.

The wolf's long and very bushy tail is a very important feature of the animal's anatomy. When a wolf curls up at night, it uses its tail to cover its feet and nose, which are gathered in the centre of the circle. The tail placed over the nose holds the warm air exhaled from the lungs over the feet and nose, warming them. The new, inhaled air filters through the tail and is

The wolf comes to water to hunt for such prey as beaver, muskrats, ducks, and geese. For convenient access to such prey, wolf dens are usually located in elevated areas overlooking a river or creek bank.

mixed and warmed by the exhaled air before it is breathed in. The vibrissae, or long whiskers, on a wolf's muzzle are organs of touch.

The dentition of the wolf consists of forty–two teeth: twelve incisors, four canines, sixteen premolars, and ten carnassials and molars. The canines of the wolf are 1–inch (2.54 centimetres) long, strong, sharp, and slightly curved. These are the teeth used for grasping prey. The wolf does not chew its food, using its carnassials to scissor off a piece of meat that can then be swallowed in a manageable chunk.

Senses

Scent plays a very important role in the life of the wolf, and it has several specialised glands, one around the anus and another on its back about 3 inches (7.6 centimetres) in front of the base of its tail. The scent from these glands is as individualistic as are our fingerprints and is used by that particular wolf as its personalised calling card.

The sense of smell in the wolf is highly developed, as would be expected in an animal possessing numerous scent glands. Research shows that wolves have been able to detect their prey at distances of up to 1.75 miles (3 kilometres). The distance at which any scent can be detected is governed by atmospheric conditions but, even under the most favourable conditions, 1.75 miles denotes a particularly keen sense of smell. The wolves usually travel until they encounter the scent of some prey species ahead of them. They then move directly toward their prey in an effort to capture it.

All canids are territorial and mark their territory with urine, faeces, and by wild scratching in the dirt. They not only mark the boundaries, they also mark the trails that they use. Their scent stations are often about 100 yards (91 metres) apart.

Wolves also have keen eyesight and are quick to detect the slightest movement of anything in front of them. Being major predators, their eyes are on the front of their heads, and they have probably a little less than 180–degree vision, unlike their prey species, which can see over 300 degrees of a circle.

Most howling is done as night falls and is often used to assemble the pack for a night's hunting. Packs also alert other packs to their whereabouts by howling.

The mournful howl of a wolf can be heard for long distances. Surrounding mountains send back echoes that prolong the sound's eerie beauty.

WINTER

Winter is the time of little light throughout the Northern Hemisphere. Within that region, from the forested areas through the taiga, then the tundra to the true Arctic, there are gradations of even less light. These are regions that have very little human population, except for the native peoples, because with the darkness comes biting, devastating cold. The most northern reaches are home to muskoxen, arctic hares, ptarmigan, arctic foxes, polar bears, lemmings, and voles. Caribou, reindeer, arctic and red foxes, ptarmigan, lemmings, and voles live on the tundra. The taiga hosts reindeer, caribou, moose, red fox, lynx, snowshoe hares, and voles. The forested region harbours moose, deer, red fox, lynx, snowshoe hares, beavers, grouse,

and voles. All of these regions are home to and last bastions of wolves, which have been extirpated from their former homes in warmer climes.

Snow Cover

Although some of the Arctic regions are considered deserts because of their minimal yearly precipitation levels, the moisture that does come down does so in the form of snow. The almost constant cold allows the snow to accumulate perpetually. This is the stuff of glaciers. The taiga and the forested regions get more snow per year, but lose their white mantle to the warm breath of the southern Chinook winds each spring. The amount of darkness has little effect upon the various creatures, yet the amount of snow does.

Long before our barometers begin to

The black phase of the grey wolf stands out very conspicuously against a white, snowy background. However, in a forested area, there are also many black trees silhouetted against the snow, which helps the black wolf to blend in.

Wolves do not have the elliptical pupils that the cats do, even though they do most of their hunting and travelling at night. Baby wolves have blue eyes that gradually turn yellow at about three months of age.

This wolf, living in the Arctic on Ellesmere Island, preys mainly upon the Peary caribou, muskoxen, arctic hares, and ptarmigan.

show changes in the atmospheric pressure, those changes have registered intuitively in all wild creatures and spurred them into action. Most will feed very heavily because a new depth of snow may force them to be inactive for prolonged periods of time. Though a new depth of snow hampers most creatures, lemmings and voles actually thrive in it because it adds another layer of protection over their heads. Having laid out an intricate network of tunnels beneath the first snow, voles eat, sleep, and carry on their daily activities in an almost predator–free world.

The wolves, driven by hunger (they are almost always driven by hunger), emerge from the mounds of snow that had been their beds. Their dense coats keep them warm in even the bitterest of weather and, as there is practically no body heat loss through their fur, none of the snow covering will have melted on them.

No matter how hungry they are, their emergence from their snowy beds is a time of excited reunion and rebonding. All of the wolves bounce and jump around, greeting each other according to his or her status. The pups and even the yearlings grovel before their parents. Tails held down but wagging, they approach the adults while holding their bodies low. They lick the adults' muzzles and are licked by the adults in return. The adults' tails are held high as befits the dominant pair. When the greetings are over, it's time to get to the work at hand—that is, it's time to eat.

When the snow reaches a depth of 18 inches (45 centimetres), it is up to the adult's chest and this makes for hard going. The wolves start out in single file, led by the Alpha, or dominant, male. Following the adults' trail allows the shorter-legged pups to keep up with little effort. Rather than journeying to a specific area to hunt a specific animal, the wolves follow the path of least resistance, travelling on windswept lakes, areas where the wind has blown the snow from the tundra grasses, and on centuries-old game trails that have

Wolves are highly intelligent animals, living well–organised social lives. The pointed ears and sharp features of this wolf highlight the intensity of its concentration.

To travel in deep snow, the wolf must bound or jump. This activity soon proves very tiring and cannot be kept up for long distances.

Unlike bears, wolves have great difficulty in standing upright upon their hind legs unless they have something to lean against.

One of the most thrilling, spine–tingling sounds in the entire world is to hear a grey wolf howl. Wolves can be made to howl quite easily, and in Canada's Algonquin Provincial Park, rangers conduct night walks on which they induce the wolves to howl, with great success.

been beaten down by the most recent animals to pass.

Hunting Tactics

Where possible, wolves will travel upwind. They have three basic methods of hunting. They will travel until they actually spot a prey species. By travelling upwind, the scent of any prey species ahead of them will be carried to them. They will then follow the air currents directly to the game. Or, they may actually follow the scent trail left by a game animal's foot tracks and body odour, no matter which way the wind is blowing. Despite the method they use, wolves prefer to approach their prey from its downwind side so that their body scent is not carried to the prey species, alerting it to their presence.

Although the wolves are cursorial hunters,

In deep snow, wolves will often follow the exact trails made by the prey species, thus conserving their own energy for the chase and kill.

able to run most prey to earth, they prefer to get as close to the animal as is possible before testing it. Spotting their prey and killing it are two very different things. Wolves eat everything from a mouse to a moose, but killing animals as large as an elk, caribou, moose, or muskox is fraught with danger.

After locating prey by sight or scent, wolves attempt to get as close as is possible before being discovered by the prey. As wolves get closer, their excitement builds, as is demonstrated by the wagging of their tails. All canines display excitement in this way. It is at this stage that the pups, in their eagerness, may spoil the hunt by wildly dashing after the prey, alerting it

before the pack has closed the distance sufficiently to make the chase successful. If there is snow on the ground, this is less likely to happen, as the wolves then follow the leader single file and the pups will have been relegated to the end of the line.

Each attack is a testing of the prey species. If wolves have not closed in on the prey after chasing it for 300 yards (273 metres) or so, the chase is usually discontinued. If the animals make a determined stand or actually charge at the wolves, they also abandon the chase.

When wolves close in on an animal, whichever wolf is close enough bites at the animal's legs or flanks. The leader then attempts to grab the animal by the nose to

Wolves have no trouble moving through snow that is about 12 inches (30.5 centimetres) in depth. However, a snow depth of 18 inches (45 centimetres) will reach to their chests, causing them to have difficulty in travelling. In deep snow, wolves travel single file.

On moonlit nights, a wolf running in and out of the shadows appears and disappears like a wraith. Wolves are primarily nocturnal animals that avoid the heat of day. They generally commence their hunting at dusk.

This wolf has eaten the ham of this white–tailed buck. The animal's bloody muzzle shows that it has just finished eating. Before sleeping, the wolf will lick its muzzle clean with its tongue.

In this scenario, two dominant wolves are already eating, and a third wolf is showing submission by its laid–back ears. It is, in effect, asking for permission to feed.

hold it still while the pack attacks. The tearing of the leg muscles soon brings the prey species crashing down so it can be killed. The dominant animals eat first. If the prey is large a number of wolves will feed at one time while the lower–ranked animals await their turns. Each animal eats all the food it can hold. In the case of a large animal, such as a moose, wolves will stay in the vicinity of the carcass until they have consumed all edible parts.

Extensive research has shown that the wolves prey primarily on the young animals of the year or on older animals that are past their prime. However, they are often depicted as being sanitary predators, feeding only on the old and the sick. This is just not true. Not only is the wolf an opportunist, it also displays decided preferences. A pack of eight wolves in the Cassiar Mountains of British Columbia that I was in daily contact with for several weeks had all but eliminated that year's caribou calf crop. In a herd of about four hundred caribou, there were only two calves left. Although most of the bulls were still in velvet, the most mature, prime bulls had peeled the velvet from their antlers. By preference, the wolves were attacking, killing, and eating these healthy mature bulls.

The snow on top of this moose carcass shows that the wolves killed the moose before the snowfall. Although only one wolf is seen, the large number of tracks indicates that a pack of wolves has visited the carcass.

Wolves do not chew their food, but tear or scissor off chunks small enough for them to swallow. They have no flat–topped molars with which to masticate food.

This wolf is feeding on a young bull moose. To obtain such large kills, wolves must hunt cooperatively in a pack.

The dominance of the white wolf at right over the black wolf is indicated by the position of their tails. A tail held high is a sign of dominance, while a tucked tail shows submission.

Unlike domestic dogs, which have two estrus periods each year, the wolf has only one. This period is determined by the seasons so that the wolf pups will be born in the warmth of springtime, when food is plentiful. This female, which has not yet come into estrus, will not accept the sexual advances of the male.

The bulbous base of the male wolf's penis expands in the female's vagina while mating, thus locking the pair together for up to thirty minutes.

The adult bull caribou weighed in the vicinity of 350 to 400 pounds (157 to 180 kilograms) each. Almost half that weight was skin, blood, bones, antlers, and entrails and their contents that the wolves did not eat. Considering that an average wolf can eat 10 to 15 pounds (4.5 to 6.75 kilograms) or more of meat per day and there was nothing edible left on any of these carcasses each day, you might think that after such a huge meal the wolves would not have to eat again for days. Not so. They could have gone days without eating, and they often do, but while the game was plentiful they killed and ate one caribou every day.

Mating

Affectionate as the wolves are, the adults become even more so as the amount of daylight, no matter how slight, increases after December 21st. The increasing daylight stimulates the wolves' pineal gland, which, in turn, triggers their pituitary

29

Wolves in the eastern part of their range feed heavily upon the white–tailed deer, while those in the west feed mainly upon the muledeer.

These copulating wolves are shown in the "locked" position. As difficult as it may seem, the animals, if disturbed, can run while fastened in this position.

gland into releasing stimulating hormones into the bloodstream. The microscopic amounts of hormones trigger a response in the wolves' activities completely out of proportion to the amount used. The females begin to enter estrus, or come into heat.

The actual timing of estrus depends upon the latitude, with the wolves in the more southern regions breeding before those in the far north. There is an actual courtship or bonding period in which the Alpha adults spend even more time together than they usually do and engage in more bodily contact. The female will have a bloody discharge from her vulva for a period of eight to ten days before estrus begins. She will be in estrus for five to seven days, during which time copulation occurs a number of times. As is true with all the canine family, the bulb at the base of the male's penis expands inside the female's vagina, locking the two animals together for a period of up to thirty minutes.

Wolves spend a lot of their time playing before they set out to hunt. This is a bonding of friendship between the animals as well as a period of stretching muscles prior to their being used in serious hunting.

Still 'hung up,' these copulating wolves are now in a position to be able to run if the need arises.

Howling is a means of communication and often a sign of exuberance. When a group of wolves howl, they start on low notes, with each succeeding howl being a little higher than the previous one.

When wolves kill a prey animal that is larger than they can consume at one time, they will sleep in the immediate vicinity and feed again when they awaken. This wolf is sleeping on top of a portion of an uneaten white-tailed deer carcass.

Grey wolves are known as cursorial hunters, being capable of running down their prey species. They are tenacious and strategic predators and, in a team situation, will take on animals as large as muskoxen and bears.

Territory and Pack Order

Wolves are territorial, with each pack living and hunting on its own particular area. The territory may change with the season because of the migration of the prey species or weather conditions, or it may stay basically the same. Although the wolves are very sociable animals, that sociability extends just to the individual pack members. Territorialism is a basic need for most predatory species because they need a given amount of food to ensure the pack's survival. The size of the territory is based upon such factors as the number of prey species that can be found in their territory, the number of animals in the individual pack, and the fighting strength of the individual members within the pack.

Where possible, different packs will set up a buffer zone, a 'no man's land', between their territories in an effort to minimise the amount of confrontation and conflict. Packs with some overlapping territory will try to avoid meeting the other pack on the same area at the same time. The whereabouts of each pack is usually announced by howling. Frequently the

game living in the buffer zone will not be hunted by the packs on either side of the zone.

According to the density of the wolves in the entire region and the amount of food available to the wolves in that region, their home range or territory may be from about 40 to 160 square miles (104 to 416 square kilometres).

To travel in deep snow, the wolf must bound or jump. This activity soon proves very tiring and cannot be kept up for long distances.

SPRING

In spring a wolf's actions are directed to the digging of a den or at least to remodelling the one that was used previously by an established pack.

Again, according to the latitude, spring can mean many things. In the far north, it may only mean the lessening of winter. In the forested areas a warm, chinook wind can turn the white, snow–laden landscape to a soggy brown morass overnight. Whereas the deepening snow had provided a safe haven for lemmings and voles, the melting snow not only evaporates their overhead cover, its liquidification floods out their tunnels and burrows, forcing them to seek sanctuary on exposed roots, stumps, rocks, and other elevated perches.

Denning and Birth

Dens are not used on a regular basis by wolves, coyotes, or red foxes. All of these canids sleep outdoors all year long and utilise a den only for the birthing and rearing of their young. Wolf dens are usually on an elevated area, on a ridge or at the top of a river or creek bank. The two requirements are an elevation above the surrounding area, if possible, and its proximity to water.

Wolf dens are usually dug in riverbanks, as is this one. The soil there is often considerably softer, making for much easier digging.

Because of their heavy fur coats, wolves are not active during the heat of a summer's day. This wolf has sought the coolness afforded by the deep shade of the forest.

A portrait of a young wolf that has sought shelter in a hollow tree. The den is used strictly for birthing and early rearing of the young, and the animals live outdoors for the rest of the year.

These wolf pups are about one month old and their eyes are still blue in colouration, though gradually they will turn yellow. When they are about twenty–eight days old, pups play among themselves to establish dominance in the pack.

The den itself usually has an oval–shaped tunnel about 15 to 24 inches (38 to 61 centimetres) wide and 3 feet (91 centimetres) high that extends back into the earth for a distance of 10 to 15 feet (3 to 4.5 metres) The tunnel ends in a chamber about 4 to 5 feet (1.2 to 1.5 metres) in diameter and 2.5 feet (75 centimetres) high. No bedding material is brought into the den by the parents. Both adults take part in the excavation of the den.

The wolf's gestation period is sixty–three days. The female hunts with the pack right up to her birthing time. Even after the evacuation of the den, the pack has wandered far and wide over its territory. Yet the den now becomes the focal point of all activities for a period of a little over two months.

A week or two before giving birth, the female stops going on the hunting forays and spends her time in or around the den. About twenty–four hours before actual parturition, she remains in the den.

A normal litter of wolf pups is five to six,

This six–week–old pup is lying outside the den. It will retreat to the den's safety at the very first sign of danger.

Wolf pups spend a lot of time playing and caressing their litter mates, which is a bonding pattern. Once they have settled their social rank, there is very little actual fighting among the pups.

Although commonly called the grey wolf, wolves come in every colour gradation from jet black to pure white. Those in the heavily forested areas have a tendency to be darker, while those in the Arctic are mainly white.

In a submissive posture, this young wolf is licking at the adult's muzzle, trying to get the adult to regurgitate some of the meat it has eaten. Wolves often make a kill 20 miles (32 kilometres) away from the den and carry the food all the way back in their stomachs to feed their young.

although as many as ten to fourteen have been recorded, as well as one instance of eighteen. The pups' births may be twenty to sixty minutes apart. As each pup is born, the female licks it to clean it off and to break the umbilical cord. At birth the pups weigh about 1 pound (.45 kilogram) and are about 14 inches (35 centimetres) long from nose tip to tail tip. Their short, woolly fur is a dark greyish brown in colour. The ears and eyes of the pups are sealed for the first eleven to fifteen days. The eyes are blue at first and gradually turn yellow. A pup's front legs are functional to the extent that it can drag itself around as it seeks its mother to nurse and for

warmth. The female warms the pups by curling around them.

The male and other members of the pack bring in food for the mother prior to her giving birth and for a period of about two months afterwards. When the pups are large enough, at about three to four weeks of age, the pack members carry food back to the the pups in their stomaches, which they then regurgitate. For the first week or so the female stays with the pups constantly, but after that she spends most of her time outside the den. At three weeks of age the pups come out of the den to bask in the sunlight, to nurse, and to play.

As soon as the male or any member of

The black phase of the common grey, or timber wolf, probably gave rise to the association of the wolf with evil. In reality, the wolf coexists harmoniously with man.

The maned wolf has exceptionally long legs, an adaptation that allows it to walk through, and to see over, the high grasses that grow on South American pampas.

Wolves feed heavily upon beavers whenever they can catch them. This wolf is examining the spot on a beaver dam that the animals use in crossing.

the pack comes in, the pups will caress his or their muzzles, which stimulates them to regurgitate what food they have eaten. If the hunt was unsuccessful, such caressing of their muzzles stimulates the adults to leave to hunt again to get the needed food. This caressing of the muzzle is also a bonding stimulus between the pup and the pack members and an exchange of affection, which is the glue that holds the pack together. Wolves travel no farther than they absolutely have to in order to secure the food needed for themselves and the pups.

From about three weeks of age on, the pups' play often turns into fights that become very rough, as each pup bites at the back of the others' necks in order to determine dominance. They usually settle into their dominant–submissive roles in a week's time, after which they still play roughly but don't actually fight. As the males are usually larger than the females, they become more dominant, with the

The maned wolf of South America feeds upon small rodents, birds, insects, and grinding vegetation. It has flat–topped molars for grinding such food, instead of the shearing carnassial teeth of the true grey wolf.

An adult maned wolf, which has just caught a rabbit, is being chased by a pup that wants to share the food.

Although this young wolf is capable of tearing meat from this deer carcass, it is still begging for food from the adult. Notice the stooped, submissive body posture of the young wolf.

The white–tailed deer is a major prey species for the grey wolves in the heavily forested regions of Minnesota, Quebec, and Ontario. Eating up to 15 pounds (6.7 kilograms) of meat per day each, a pack of six to eight wolves would have to kill a deer every other day to be sated.

largest male holding the number one rank. So long as all of the pups remain in good health, their ranking usually remains the same. If one of the pups is injured, no matter how slightly, its ranking will change. Each pup or adult wolf's rank is determined by what position it can physically maintain.

Food Sources

Although the young of the deer, elk, caribou, reindeer, and moose are still the sta- ples of the wolf's diet, all living flesh is grist for their mill. Over most of the wolf's range, throughout the world, the number of voles, lemmings, and ground squirrels is beyond calculation. Although a wolf may be looking for a caribou, it may fill up on ground squirrels before discovering any of the larger game.

Willow ptarmigan are very common on the tundra all across the continent, while the spruce and ruffed grouse are found in the forested regions. The young of these

These wolves will completely consume this 125–pound (56– kilogram) white–tailed deer in two to three days, sleeping between feeding periods.

birds can't fly well until they are about two weeks old. A wolf running into a covey of grouse and chicks can just literally scoop up all that it finds.

To protect themselves from wolf attacks, muskoxen developed the defensive circle. When pursued by wolves, the animals form a protective circle with all of their heavily horned heads facing outwards and the young in the middle. Any wolf that gets too close may provoke a charge from one of the adult bulls. The charge is only for a short distance, as even the bulls don't want to get too far from the protective circle. While this circle has long provided an adequate defence against the wolves, it was the the muskoxen's undoing when confronted by modern man and guns.

The huge buffalo wolf is extinct in the wild, along with the vast herds of buffalo. These wolves used to follow the buffalo

and attempt to catch a straggler or some old or sick animal. The wolves were too smart to attempt to cut a calf from the protection of the herd, which would charge en masse.

Elk and caribou are both herd animals, but their strategies for protection are different. However, it must be remembered that the elk is a larger animal than the caribou. Elk travel in small bands of perhaps five to twenty–five animals. Caribou travel in herds that may number into the thousands.

When elk are attacked, they may either flee or the irate cows may attack. Elk calves are almost never left alone. Cows without calves, aunties, guard the calves if their mothers are off feeding.

Caribou depend upon their speed to outrun the wolves, and the massed herd makes it difficult for the wolves to concen-

Although wolves often hunt small animals like voles, lemmings, and ground squirrels by themselves, they tend to hunt the larger animals—including caribou, elk, and muskoxen—in a pack.

All of the canids pant in warm weather in an effort to expel as much body heat through the lungs as possible. The lolling tongue also is a thermoregulation device, cooling the blood slightly as it is exposed to the air by the tongue.

trate on one single animal. That's why birds flock, fish school, and animals herd up. There is safety in numbers. It is the stray caribou that is singled out for an attack by the pack.

One healthy wolf cannot catch one healthy caribou, and the caribou know this. It is only the caribou on the outskirts of the herd that are concerned when the wolves appear, and their best defence is to run into the middle of the herd.

In the northern forest, the wolves feed mainly upon moose. As mentioned earlier, any determined stand by these big animals is usually enough to defeat most of the wolves' attacks. Wolves do feed on the moose regularly, but they usually take the ones that run. Any creature that runs from any predator stimulates the predator's attack instincts.

Cow moose are just as dangerous as are

Wolves don't hesitate to get wet, but are quick to shake the water from their fur as soon as they get out on land. A wolf's coat of fur is so dense that, even when it swims, the water doesn't usually penetrate to its skin.

Wolves often follow the paths of rivers, as these are natural highways that make for swifter travelling.

Wolves cannot drink by suction as we humans do. Instead, they curl their tongues up and inwards and use that as a receptacle to lap water into their mouths so that it can be swallowed.

Wolves run in a rotary pattern with the right front foot coming down first, followed by the left front foot. Then the right hind foot hits the ground, followed by the left hind foot.

Over most of their range, wolves have a ready access to water. They usually locate their birthing dens close to a steady source of water so that it will be easily available to the pups.

the big bulls because even the bulls only have their antlers for part of the year. Their main attack weapons are their huge front hooves. A cow moose whose calves are threatened becomes a crashing, slashing juggernaut.

However, the most determined stand by a cow moose can be thwarted by a pack of wolves because, while some of the wolves attack one calf, others will attack the second calf. Not even a cow moose can be in two places at one time, and sooner or later one, if not both, of the calves will be pulled down and killed.

A wolf crossing an area that has been flooded by beavers is on the alert for this prey animal. Beavers live in domed lodges made of piled-up wood covered with mud. The mud freezes in the winter to the consistency of concrete, affording the animals warmth and protection.

Frogs and fish are among the wolf's foods. However, in cold weather it feeds principally on big game animals because the energy expenditure yields greater results.

SUMMER

Summer in the far north is a time of endless growth. It's not that the days are endless, because they are not. The days of summer are numbered, and the number is smaller the farther north you go. It's just that the days run into one another, and it's hard to remember where one ends and the next one starts. The sun doesn't really set––it just dips toward the horizon in acknowledgment of the passage of time.

At this time, the caribou seek out the ridges on the north–south gravelly eskers, where the constant wind helps to hold the insect hordes at bay. In some of the gullies and on the north side of the ridges, rem-

Wolves often go into the water simply to play and watch the water splash, and also to cool off on hot summer days.

nants of last year's snow attracts the caribou, who seek out the snow to cool off and to get relief from the insects.

It is for these same reasons that the wolves seek out whatever high places are in their area. Elevated vantage points are also good spots to keep track of the movements of game.

In Denali, the wolves also feed upon the Dall's sheep, capturing them when they move from their winter to summer mountain ranges.

Growing Pups

Wolf pups are usually weaned by the time they are five weeks old. The young are still using the den but, by this time, the

Surrounded by flowers, a wolf is comfortable in its short summer coat. The summer coat mainly functions as protection against insects.

Curiosity is a sign of intelligence, and this black wolf was very inquisitive about the photographer who was taking its picture.

While the wolf on the left sniffs the air for scent, the wolf on the right is checking out a urine scent station.

Young wolves leave the birthing den when they are several months old and will stay at a "rendezvous" area, which is usually located a lot closer to where the adult wolves are hunting.

Wolves live in a great variety of habitats, from Arctic icelands, to open tundra, to dense forest. At one time, they were common on the grasslands and plains of the United States.

mother will again be out hunting with the pack for food. The pups are seldom left entirely alone; usually some other member of the pack will 'babysit' the pups while the mother is out hunting.

The young adult wolves are as solicitous of the pups' welfare as are the parents; they will feed them, guard them, and play with them. As wolf pups are a study in perpetual motion, all of the members of the pack put up with a lot of puppy abuse.

At about eight weeks of age, the wolves abandon their dens for that year and move to one of what are known as 'rendezvous' sites. These areas are more centrally located to the areas in which the adults are doing most of their hunting. This saves the adults much time and travel in bringing food back to the pups. If a large kill is made, the pups may follow the pack to the kill.

By this two–month–old mark, the pups are experiencing very rapid body growth and will weigh 15 to 20 pounds (6.75 to 9 kilograms). They romp and play, stalk one another, and generally enjoy themselves. These are the most carefree months of their lives. They may wander off a short distance to hunt for mice and voles, but they are still dependent on the food brought in to them and the center of all of their activities is the rendezvous site.

Survival Tactics

Wolves don't really have many mortal enemies except man. The pups, when they first come out of the den until they are about six weeks old, may be preyed upon by golden eagles.

Grizzly bears on the tundra and polar bears in the Arctic prey upon young wolves when they can catch them. It is primarily because of the bears that the wolves don't leave their pups unattended. There are several records of a number of wolves decoying bears away from their pups' den by harassing the bears until

Wolves are capable of jumping over obstacles as high as 4 to 5 feet (1.2 to 1.5 metres) with ease, as this wolf is doing, leaping over a fallen tree.

The markings on this wolf's face are quite unusual and very attractive. The vibrissae, or long whiskers, on its muzzle are organs of touch.

they left. By teamwork, the wolves can accomplish what they couldn't alone or in pairs.

Howling

Howling is a major means of communication, and we can only surmise and try to deduce all of the messages that are being sent and received. Wolves howl to assemble the pack and to notify other packs of their whereabouts. They undoubtedly howl just for the sheer joy of it. They may howl out of loneliness when seeking a mate. Each wolf howls a little differently, and each wolf has quite a repertoire of howling.

When a pack of wolves starts to howl, its range of notes in each howl generally gets higher the longer the pack howls and as more members join in. A chorus of wolves is one of the most unforgettable sounds in the world.

Warm–Weather Habits

The bulk of wolves' activities take place at night. This is not so much of a reluctance on their part to be out while it is light as it is to avoid the heat of the day. In

Wolves respond very differently to man, according to whatever situations they have experienced. This wolf stopped without running off when he discovered the photographer across the pond. Though many people fear the wolf, it is revealing to note that there has not been a single authenticated attack by a healthy wolf on a person in North America.

the far north it is light from twenty to twenty–four hours a day, and so the activity of the wolves can be seen and documented. That far north the days are usually cooler, so the wolves are not subjected to as much daytime heat. When it does get hot, and occasionally it does, the wolves simply seek out whatever deep shade is available and remain inactive. To cool down, they often dig a bed in damp soil. Wolves also expel a lot of their internal body heat by panting very rapidly.

In the forested areas of Ontario, Minnesota, and nearby locales, the wolves remain inactive all day, as temperatures sometimes climb into the low 90 degree F (low 30 degree C) range. Near dusk they

begin to stir and start their hunting in the cool of early evening. The wolves of the forest don't have to travel as far as do the tundra wolves because they feed on a greater variety of prey, such as beavers, snowshoe hares, deer, and moose calves. All of these prey species are scattered throughout the entire region in a much more uniform pattern. There may be large areas of the tundra region that are practically devoid of wildlife, while other areas support large herds. That means that the tundra wolf has to travel long distances to find food.

Alaskan summers can be very rainy, which lowers the temperatures, so the wolves are often active throughout the

Wolves walk, trot, and lope. This wolf is loping or galloping. Wolves have been clocked at better than 40 miles (64 kilometres) per hour, but they can't keep it up for long distances. For long–distance travel, the wolves trot at a fast and steady pace.

Wolves live in a world of scent and have urine scent posts scattered throughout their entire territory, which is their claim to ownership. They often scratch vigorously after urinating. These long, deep scratch marks are a visual sign of communication.

Wolves howl to prevent other packs from trespassing on their territory. This is a natural mechanism for keeping peace among packs.

Wolves don't bark as much as coyotes do while howling, but they do bark when threatened or when they are warning another animal. Wolves will even bark at any bear that has got too close to their den site. Even though bears are much bigger and stronger than wolves, they actually fear the canids when they are in a pack.

Running at full speed, grey wolves can easily overtake many species. They have been known to attain a speed of better than 40 miles (64 kilometres) per hour.

entire day. I have observed that rain does not seem to faze the wolves at all. They usually follow the gravel bars and riverbeds; these natural highways offer a travel lane of the least resistance. The wolves are constantly wading back and forth across the shallow rivers and occasionally have to swim. Being wet is part of being a wolf in Alaska. Feeding on meat, wolves get a lot of their daily water requirements from the animals' blood. They drink water when the opportunity presents itself, while in the winter they slake their thirst with snow.

A grey wolf runs easily through water. In summer, wolves drink water whenever the opportunity arises; in winter, they obtain water from snow.

A wolf running very fast easily closes in on most prey. If it has not caught the animal within 300 yards (273 metres), it will likely abandon the chase.

Curling up its lips to reveal its large canine teeth and laying back its ears, this dominant wolf is displaying aggression.

In pursuit of prey, wolves readily cross small brooks, streams, and rivers. They have even been seen venturing out into lakes to attack swimming animals.

Wolves have a very keen sense of hearing and are able to detect another wolf howl from a distance of several miles. Because each wolf's howl is distinctive, individuals can be identified through their voices.

AUTUMN

Autumn starts early in wolf country. The first part of September finds the tundra region aflame with bright reds, oranges, and yellows. The leaves of the dwarf birches and blueberry bushes blaze like the Biblical burning bush. Each day the hues get brighter and the mosaic becomes more spectacular.

In the taiga, the aspens are the most common deciduous trees, and in their glory days their leaves shimmer like beaten goldleaf. On their long stems, the leaves twist, turn, and vibrate as they are set in motion by each passing breeze.

Winter Preparations

Early morning (there is a night and day now) often finds the leaves rimmed with frost. Each day it takes the sun a little longer to beat back the cold of the night and to melt the frost. All creatures know instinctively that winter will soon win out.

The wolf's coat becomes deep and dense, with the result that, as long as the wind does not blow too strongly, the animal is impervious to the cold.

Everything awaits the coming of the first snow—and nothing has to wait too long. The mountaintops had received their first dusting of snow weeks before, and each successive storm powdered the mountains at a lower level.

The wolf pups know about snow instinctively, yet such inner knowledge does not detract from, nor inhibit, the sheer exuberance they display as they dash about in the powdery fluff.

The wolf inhabits vast areas. Depending upon the availability of food, a pack's territory may range from 10 to 100 square miles (26 to 260 square kilometres) or more.

The grey wolf resided in North American long before the first Indians and Eskimos came across Beringia, eighteen thousand years ago.

Packs and Migration

The pups have been following the pack on their excursions afield to hunt. They have much to learn, and even their eagerness does not make up for their lack of size, weight, and strength. In late September they will weigh in the vicinity of 50 pounds (22.5 kilograms) and will not reach their full size for months to come.

Hunting big game is a hazardous business. Wolves are often gored or stomped on by the animals they hunt. Often they simply miscalculate and are struck by a running animal's hoof. A bone broken by accident is just as broken as if it were done deliberately, and anything that incapacitates a wolf is a threat to its life.

Within each pack, with each individual, a crippled animal's fate is different. In all packs, in all animal societies, a crippled animal loses its rank or status within the hierarchy. If the Alpha wolf is badly crippled, he may fall to the lowest rank of all. In some cases the crippled animal may be cared for. In most cases all of the other animals move up one notch in their society, and all may turn on the crippled animal and drive it from the pack. In extreme

Although the wolf's diet is about ninety–eight percent meat, it occasionally consumes a little grass—evidently for its cathartic value—and a few insects. This wolf is eating bark beetles.

cases all of the animals may turn on the injured one and kill it. Nature is a realist; it has no place for niceties.

If the injured animal remains with the pack and recovers from its injuries, it will have to fight its way back up the social ladder. The status at any level is not a given position, but is the highest one that individual animal can take and hold. In the animal world, might does make right. It is not the fate of an individual animal that matters; it is the survival of the pack that does.

Prior to their breeding season in late September, the caribou herds will reverse themselves and leave the barren, wind–swept tundra region for the greater protection of the taiga. Most of the wolf packs follow along. The predator must stay close to the prey species. Except for some muskox herds in the far north, most of the tundra regions are devoid of animals large enough to support a wolf pack.

Autumn is the natural dispersal time for most wild creatures. Winter is coming on and food for all active species will be harder to come by. To avoid conflict over food, and later over breeding rights or their suppression, the young of many species strike off on their own. In the case of the wolves, it is the two–and–a–half–year–old adults that may leave to find mates and to start packs of their own.

It is the dispersal of the young that usually expands the range of any species that is increasing in population. In wolves, the established packs usually occupy the best territory containing the most game. Young

Wolves are keenly alert to every sound made by every creature around them. This wolf is attentive to a noise in the distance.

71

wolves, starting out as just a pair, are thus forced to go into new areas or must utilise poorer, unused areas in regular wolf areas or move into the buffer zone between two established packs. Sometimes the adult wolves will allow their offspring to establish a pack of their own on some of their own territory.

Nature abhors a vacuum. Nothing in nature is static. Although some den sites may be utilised for many, many years, the size of the pack's territory around the den site may fluctuate dramatically according to the size of the pack utilising the den and the amount of prey animals available to the pack.

Wolf Populations

In different locations, in different countries around the world, the wolf today is being hunted, being protected, or being

Although the grey wolf is this animal's most widely accepted common name, it is also called timber wolf, arctic wolf, and buffalo wolf, among other names. Such common names refer to the particular areas in which they are found.

These two wolves are a good illustration of several of the different colour phases of the grey wolf. Often such dimorphism is found among the puppies of just one litter.

A pair of typical grey, or timber, wolves display their most commonly seen colouration. Beneath their grey, white, and black hairs is a base coat of yellow.

The Alpha, or dominant, pair of wolves tolerates the presence of the third wolf because its submissive body language indicates that it knows its place in the social system.

In the north country, wolves constantly have to cross streams and rivers. They take to the water without hesitation and swim readily, following caribou wherever they go.

Notice the wide, teardrop–shaped mane over the wolf's shoulders that extends down its back. When angered or frightened, erectorpili muscles cause this mane to stand erect, making the wolf look much larger than it is in reality.

It is very easy to see the close resemblance between this grey wolf and a German shepherd. The wolf's head, however, is broader than the dog's.

argued about. In some areas where the populations are high, their numbers are being controlled by various methods. In places where the population is low, wolves are being given partial or complete protection. In still other places, the wolf is being reintroduced after having been completely eliminated in prior years. All of these programs have merit, and it is not the intention of the author to discuss the aspects of each.

There is a very interesting footnote that is little known. In areas where the wolf is heavily controlled, its population may actually increase because of man's activities. Under normal conditions, only the Alpha members of the pack breed. There may be up to a dozen wolves in the pack that are mature enough to breed, but all such activity in the pack is restricted to and by the Alpha wolves.

If a number of the wolves are removed from the pack, including the Alpha pair, the pack may scatter and break down into a number of smaller units. Whereas only the Alpha pair out of twelve wolves may have bred previously, after the breakup three pairs may breed, with each of the smaller packs using part of the territory held by the larger, original pack. Thus, in an area that previously produced six pups in a given year, eighteen might now be produced. The only constraints placed on each rapid population explosion will be the number of prey animals in the area available to the wolves, and man.

All–white wolves are common in the Arctic, but they can be found in many types of habitat. Their white coats help them to blend in with the snow, but also make them very conspicuous against a darker background.

The faces of most wolves are lighter in colouration than are their bodies. Numerous markings may occur, and body hair can range from black to salt–and–pepper grey to white.

AFTERWORD

This subordinate wolf is mouthing the muzzle of the dominant Alpha male. This is a sign of submission. It is also a gesture used by wolf pups when they want adult wolves to disgorge food for them to eat.

The attitude of man toward the wolf has undergone a tremendous change in recent years in most of the world. Extensive comprehensive studies have brought a vast amount of new knowledge, of true knowledge, to light.

The wolf is a true symbol of the wilderness; it can live only in the wilderness. In the wolf's natural state it lives in balance with its prey species. The fluctuation in the population of either predator or prey either causes or reflects a fluctuation in the other. No predator wipes out its prey species. As such, the wolf is a good barometer of our environment. Recent studies have proven that in areas where wolves prey upon deer, both the quality of the habitat and the general health of the deer herd are improved.

The arguments, both pro and con, will continue to swirl around the wolf controversy for years to come. I believe that our greatest cause for alarm is our burgeoning human population and our intrusion and destruction of the wilderness. As the wilderness goes, so goes the wolf. I, for one, don't want to live without either.

PHOTO CREDITS